CHEWING GUM
by Norma E. Lee

Illustrated by Marvin Friedman
Prentice-Hall, Inc., Englewood Cliffs, N.J.

Printed in the United States of America   •J

Prentice-Hall International, Inc., London
Prentice-Hall of Australia, Pty. Ltd., North Sydney
Prentice-Hall of Canada, Ltd., Toronto
Prentice-Hall of India Private Ltd., New Delhi
Prentice-Hall of Japan, Inc., Tokyo

Prentice-Hall, Inc., Englewood Cliffs, New Jersey

**Library of Congress Cataloging in Publication
Data**

Lee, Norma.
    Chewing gum.

    SUMMARY: Discusses the development of
chewing gum from homemade to commercial
product and its social acceptance throughout
the world.
    1. Chewing gum—Juvenile literature.
[1. Chewing gum]   I. Friedman, Marvin.
II. Title.
TX799.L43   664'.6   75–12760
ISBN 0–13–129601–9

10   9   8   7   6   5   4   3   2   1

To my children

The first Americans chewed chewing gum. Wampanoag Indians introduced gum chewing to the Pilgrims. Their gum was only wads of resin sticking to spruce trees. It was waxy and tough, but the Pilgrims liked spruce gum.

When they couldn't find gum on spruce trees, Pilgrims bought some at the store. Sometimes they chewed grains or grasses or fingernails. Everyone, even farmers, wanted something to chew.

Thousands of settlers arrived in America, but for more than 200 years, there was only one chewing gum—spruce gum.

Paraffin was discovered in 1830, and Americans found out it was chewable. Our first paraffin came from English coal mines. Soon we learned how to manufacture it and to flavor the tasteless chew.

Pioneers' wagons rolled westward. Settlers in Oklahoma and Missouri learned about another chewing gum from the

Osage Indians. For thousands of years, ancestors of the Osage had chewed chicle.

Chicle is the hardened sap of sapodilla trees that grow in Central America. It was the chewiest chewing gum yet.

A Mexican, General Antonio Lopez de Santa Anna, had an idea concerning chicle. He thought it might be made into a substitute for rubber. In 1869 he brought some chicle samples to Thomas Adams, an American inventor.

Attempts to make the rubber failed, but Mr. Adams had another idea about chicle. In 1875 he marketed the first chicle-based chewing gum.

Chicle chewing gum was good, and it began getting better. Gum chewers discovered new flavors and some remarkable qualities of chewing gum.

In 1906 gum manufacturers added paraffin to chicle base and gave America something to sing about.

During World War I, weary soldiers chewed gum because chewing kept them alert.

Baseball players chewed gum before and during games.
When they were tense, chewing calmed them.

Will Rogers, a popular entertainer during the 20s and 30s, amused Americans. In a favorite act the cowboy from Oklahoma presented a rope-twirling performance while chewing chewing gum.

GIRLFRIEND IS SO FAT SHE CAN
SWER THE FRONT DOOR WITHOUT LEAVING
HE KITCHEN
SNAP
SNAP
CHOMP
CHOMP

In the 1940s millions of Americans worked in factories to help end World War II. Sometimes their jobs were dull and uninteresting. They thought that chewing gum made the work easier.

Dentists and dieters welcomed sugarless gum in the late 1940s.

Early jet plane travel, in the 1950s, alerted us to still another chewing gum benefit. Chewing relieves discomfort in passengers' ears, caused by varying air pressures, while flying in unpressurized cabins.

Mothers know that certain medicines taste better when they are made into chewing gum.

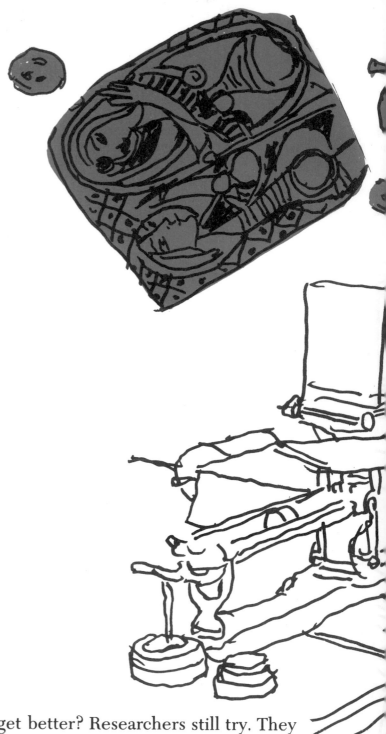

Can chewing gum get better? Researchers still try. They are developing gum that will not stick to dentures and, perhaps, bubbles that glow in the dark!

Americans of all ages like chewing gum.

When you chew gum, remember:

    1. Don't chew in places where chewing will disturb others.

    2. Never chew noisily or with your mouth open.

3. Don't chew in the presence of others without offering them some gum.

4. Wrap your chewing gum in paper before disposing of it.